MICROWAVE COOKING

Margaret Weale

CHA

CONTENTS

First published in Great Britain in 1985
This edition published in 1994 by Chancellor Press
an imprint of Reed Consumer Books Limited
Michelin House, 81 Fulham Road, London SW3 6RB
and Auckland, Melbourne, Singapore and Toronto

Copyright © 1985 Reed International Books Limited

ISBN 1 85152 511 4

A CIP catalogue record for this book is available
from the British Library

Printed in China

INTRODUCTION

More and more people are now enjoying the benefits of microwave cooking. This relatively new domestic appliance is proving a boon to busy Mums, career women and single people – to everyone who leads a full life.

Not only is a microwave oven great for defrosting frozen food or reheating cooked food, but it is also a cooker in its own right, capable of cooking a wide variety of foods to perfection, often in a fraction of the time it takes to cook them conventionally.

It is not intended to replace the conventional cooker, which is still needed to cook such foods as roast potatoes, Yorkshire puddings, soufflés and double-crust pies, as well as for deep-frying and boiling eggs. But used with your ordinary cooker and freezer, a microwave oven enables you to provide a variety of menus in the minimum time. Make full use too of the wide range of excellent canned and packaged foods now available and you can reduce the time spent in the kitchen still further.

This book aims to provide a variety of recipes, using all types of foods, to suit different microwave oven owners. Read the basic information first to ensure success every time, then discover for yourself just how easy microwave cooking is. It's almost like having another pair of hands in the kitchen!

NOTES

Standard spoon measurements are used in all recipes.
1 tablespoon = one 15 ml spoon
1 teaspoon = one 5 ml spoon
All spoon measures are level.

Fresh herbs are used unless otherwise stated. If unobtainable substitute a bouquet garni of the equivalent dried herbs, or use dried herbs instead but halve the quantities stated.

Use freshly ground black pepper where pepper is specified.

For all recipes, quantities are given in both metric and imperial measures. Follow either set but not a mixture of both, because they are not interchangeable.

BASIC COOKING TECHNIQUES

Timing
Correct timing is essential for successful results, and the golden rule in microwave cooking is to under-cook rather than risk over-cooking. Under-cooked food can always be returned to the oven for further cooking, but there is no remedy for over-cooked, spoilt food. Look as you cook, inspect food regularly, and always under-estimate rather than over-estimate the time required. Times given throughout this book for defrosting, reheating and cooking food should be used as a guide only; ovens do vary from one model to another and manufacturer's instructions should be followed. In addition, several factors related to the food itself will affect timing.

The quantity of food: The more food you put in the oven, the longer it will take to cook. For instance, two jacket potatoes will take longer to cook than one. Generally when you double the amount of food the cooking time is increased by between one third and one half. Similarly, if you halve the amount of food in a given recipe, the cooking time should be just over half the given time.

Density: Dense foods such as meat will take longer to heat and cook than porous, light-textured foods such as bread, cakes, pastry and puddings.

Moisture content: The more moisture food contains, the longer it will take to cook.

Thickness and shape of food: Since microwaves penetrate food to a depth of about 3.5 cm (1½ inches), thinner or smaller pieces will cook faster than thicker or larger pieces of the same food. A regular shape will cook more evenly, so it is advisable to bone and roll irregular shaped joints of meat.

Size and shape of cooking dish: Food placed in a small deep dish takes longer to cook than the same amount of food placed in a larger, more shallow dish.

Starting temperature of food: Food taken straight from the refrigerator will take longer to cook than food at room temperature. Similarly, frozen food takes longer to cook than refrigerated food. Room temperatures vary according to the season, so cooking times should be slightly longer on cold days.

Personal preference: Times given can be increased or decreased according to taste.

Shielding Food
Shield the inner, narrower tail end pieces of whole fish or the tips of poultry legs and wings with small smooth pieces of foil to slow down their rate of cooking.

Protect the thin end of a leg of lamb with foil for about half the cooking time, to prevent over-cooking.

Never allow foil to touch any part of the oven interior.

Stirring and Turning

Since microwaves start cooking food around the outside first, it is often necessary to stir or turn food during cooking to give more even cooking results.

When food in a dish is to be stirred, the outer portions should be brought to the centre and the less cooked centre portions moved to the outside of the dish.

Joints of meat and poultry, or thick pieces of meat and fish, should be turned over during defrosting, reheating and cooking.

If your microwave oven does not have a turntable, it is often advisable to rotate dishes during cooking, especially if the contents cannot be stirred.

Food Arrangement

The arrangement of food in the oven is important whether you are defrosting, reheating or cooking. For even results, food should be of similar height, avoiding mounds, especially in the centre. Always place the thicker, denser parts towards the outside of the dish; for example, when cooking chicken drumsticks, arrange the meatier parts around the outside of the dish and the thinner ends towards the centre.

Covering Food

Many foods are covered during cooking to retain steam and moisture. Clingfilm forms a tighter seal than a loose lid and can speed up the cooking process. It should be used for all recipe instructions in this book that say 'cover', unless otherwise specified, but do not use it wrapped directly around food for microwaving. Always use clingfilm that is labelled specifically for use in the microwave, and always refer to package instructions.

Food which splatters during cooking can be covered with kitchen or greaseproof paper. Do not cover foods you wish to keep dry. To reheat bread or pastry, place on kitchen paper and lay more paper on top to absorb moisture and prevent sogginess.

Food with Shells, Skin or Membrane

Do not try to boil eggs unless the manufacturer recommends a special way of doing this, as pressure will build up inside the shell and cause the egg to explode.

Whole foods with skin, such as potatoes, should be pricked all over to prevent bursting.

The membrane covering egg yolks should be pierced gently before placing in the oven.

Browning

Microwave cooking is very fast. It is also a moist form of cooking. Because of this, many foods do not brown.

Larger joints of meat and whole chickens or turkeys will brown during their longer time in the oven, but the skin will not crisp.

Cooking small joints of meat or poultry in pierced roasting bags encourages browning.

Smaller pieces of meat, such as chops or steaks, can be browned by cooking them on a special *microwave browning dish* (see page 12).

The colour of meat can be enhanced by brushing it with soy sauce or Worcestershire sauce, or by sprinkling on special microwave seasonings, before cooking.

You can, of course, fry meat conventionally before cooking in a microwave oven to seal and brown, while dishes with a topping which is normally browned can be finished off under a preheated conventional grill.

Standing Time

All food continues to cook after it has been removed from a microwave oven. The food is no longer being cooked by microwaves but by the conduction of heat towards the centre. It is a necessary part of the cooking process and must be taken into consideration when timing and checking food for readiness, to prevent over-cooking.

Test food for readiness after the standing time recommended in these recipes. If no standing time is required, test immediately after removing from the oven.

COOKING CONTAINERS

You can use a far wider variety of cooking containers in a microwave oven than in a conventional oven. You will not, of course, use metal pans or baking tins, but will use some materials which you have never used in an oven before, such as kitchen paper, paper napkins and special plastics.

Testing Containers
If in doubt, always test a container to see if it is suitable for microwave oven use. To do this, simply place a glass of water in the container and microwave on HIGH for 1 minute: if the water is warm and the dish is cool then it is suitable to use; if the water is cold and the dish is hot it is unsuitable. When the dish is slightly warm this means that it is absorbing some microwave energy and, although it may be safe to use, it is likely to slow down the rate of cooking and the overall cooking time may have to be increased.

China and Pottery: Sturdy china dishes without metal trims are suitable. Some pottery and earthenware can be used, but if it is porous and contains moisture, it can rob the food of microwave energy, resulting in longer cooking times; it will also get hot.

Glass: Ovenproof glass or glass ceramic dishes are widely used in microwave cooking. Clear glass dishes such as Pyrex are particularly suitable because you can actually see how the food is cooking. Glass which is not ovenproof, lead crystal or antique glass should be avoided.

Metal: Generally speaking metal containers and utensils should not be used in a microwave oven; this includes china and glass with a metal trim or signature on the base. There are, however, exceptions to every rule. Food packed in foil containers less than 1.5 cm (¾ inch) deep may be used, *provided they do not touch the oven interior*, because they are shallow enough to allow microwaves to penetrate food from the top. Foil-lined containers should not be placed in the oven.

Foil wrappings on butter should be removed and metal twist ties should be replaced by plastic ones, string or elastic bands. Replace metal skewers with wooden skewers or cocktail sticks.

Paper: Paper cups, plates, towels and napkins can all be used in a microwave oven, although prolonged heating in the oven can cause paper to burn. Napkins should be white, because colour could be transferred to food. Plastic-coated paper plates should not be used unless they are labelled for microwave oven use.

Greaseproof paper can be used as a loose covering, but never use waxed paper because the wax will melt. Kitchen paper is useful for absorbing moisture and fat, and for reheating bread and pastry products.

Plastics: Dishwasher-safe rigid plastic containers can be used for low temperature short-term cooking, but they should not be

used to heat or cook foods with a high fat or sugar content.

Tupperware and melamine are not recommended. Plastic baby bottles can be used to warm milk. Clingfilm makes a good tight seal when dishes are to be covered (see page 8).

Plastic pouches containing commercially prepared foods can be slit and placed on a plate in the oven. Pierced roasting bags are useful for cooking meat, poultry and vegetables.

Straw and Wood: Straw and wicker baskets can be used for the very short times needed to heat bread rolls.

Small utensils, such as wooden spoons, can be left in the oven for short periods, e.g. when making sauces.

If wood is used for prolonged cooking, the moisture evaporates from it and cracking will result.

Choosing the Best Size and Shape of Cooking Container

Always choose a container which fits the food. The shape and size of the container and the depth of food in it will not only affect the cooking time but also the attention required during cooking, and the end result.

Containers should be large enough to prevent spillage. Round dishes are best for even heating and cooking. Square dishes should have rounded corners to prevent over-cooking in these areas. Rectangular containers are least successful. Straight sided dishes are preferable to those with sloping sides.

Ring moulds give good results and are especially good for food that cannot be stirred. If you do not have a ring mould, improvise by placing a tumbler or glass jar in the centre of a suitable dish.

Meat Thermometers

Use only special microwave meat thermometers inside the oven during cooking. If you don't have one of these, remove joint from the oven to test with an ordinary meat thermometer or metal skewer in the usual way, until the meat juices run clear.

Microwave Browning Dish

This has been specially designed to brown food in a microwave oven. It is made of a ceramic material with a coating on the underside which absorbs microwave energy. The empty dish is preheated in the oven until the bottom surface is very hot so that the food placed on it is seared and browned. Always follow the manufacturer's instructions for preheating and cooking times, and use oven gloves to handle the dish.

Special Microwave Containers and Utensils

There is now an ever-increasing variety of cooking containers, utensils and accessories on the market, specially designed for microwave oven use. Some can be used in conventional ovens and freezers, too.

TIME SAVERS

Use the HIGH setting on your oven when following these tips:
- Heat citrus fruits for 30 seconds. They will be easier to squeeze, and will give more juice.
- Soften butter, cheese spread or cream cheese in 15 seconds to make them more spreadable.
- Heat syrup in a jug for easier measuring and pouring.
- Dry herbs by heating them on kitchen paper until they are dry and crumbly. Times will vary according to quantity and variety of herb. Check at 30 second intervals.
- Toast blanched almonds: place 125 g (4 oz) almonds in a dish with 25 g (1 oz) butter and heat for a few minutes until lightly browned, stirring regularly.
- Dissolve gelatine in water in seconds.
- Speed up barbecue cooking by partly cooking food in the oven before placing over the hot coals.
- Melt 125 g (4 oz) chocolate in a bowl in 1½ minutes. Stir after 1 minute.
- Dissolve packet jellies: cut into pieces, place in a bowl with 300 ml (½ pint) water and heat for 1½ to 2 minutes, stirring after 1 minute. Stir well and make up to 600 ml (1 pint) with ice cubes and cold water.
- Prove bread dough in less time. Place in a covered bowl and microwave for 15 seconds. Leave to stand for 5 to 10 minutes. Repeat until the dough has doubled in size.

SAFETY AND MAINTENANCE

A microwave oven is one of the safest appliances in the kitchen, for it has no hot surfaces inside or outside. Dishes used for cooking only get hot due to heat being conducted from the hot food.

If you are about to buy a microwave oven, buy one which carries the BEAB (British Electrotechnical Approvals Board) Mark of Safety or the Electricity Council's Approved for Safety label. This means that a sample of the appliance has been thoroughly tested for electrical safety and microwave leakage.

All microwave ovens are designed so that a safety mechanism ensures that the oven cannot operate until the door has been tightly closed and the appropriate control has been switched on. As soon as the door is opened the oven switches off and will not start again until the door is securely closed.

The microwave oven must be one of the easiest kitchen appliances to keep clean. Usually all that is necessary is to wipe over the inside and outside after each use. Do not use abrasives or strong cleaning agents. Pay particular attention to the door area and door seal and ensure that food splashes are removed. If any soiling proves difficult to remove from the interior, simply heat a small container of water in the oven until boiling; the moisture will loosen the soil which can then be removed with a damp cloth.

If smells build up inside the oven after cooking strong-smelling food, place a cup or bowl containing three parts water to one part lemon juice in the oven and boil for a few minutes.

Have the oven serviced regularly, by a qualified service engineer, as recommended by the manufacturer.

OVEN OUTPUT

The higher the power output of an oven, the faster it will cook. Most ovens now have at least two settings which allow you to cook quickly on HIGH/FULL POWER and to defrost or cook more slowly on a lower LOW/DEFROST setting. Some ovens have variable power which provides a wider variety of settings.

The recipes and times given in this book have been tested in ovens with maximum power output levels of 600W to 700W and a LOW setting of 200W to 300W. Only two settings are used and they represent the power output levels most readily available, by whatever name or number, on most ovens.

Ovens with Lower Output

Ovens with a maximum output of less than 600W will take longer to defrost, reheat and cook food. The following chart will enable you to adjust the times given in this book, but it is also important to follow the manufacturer's recommended times.

Cooking Time in 600W–700W ovens	Increased Time in 500W–600W ovens
30 secs	35 secs
1 min	1 min 9 secs
2 mins	2 mins 22 secs
3 mins	3 mins 27 secs
4 mins	4 mins 36 secs
5 mins	5 mins 45 secs
10 mins	11 mins 30 secs
15 mins	17 mins 15 secs
20 mins	23 mins
25 mins	28 mins 45 secs
30 mins	34 mins 30 secs

Defrosting Guide

Food	Quantity or Weight	Time on LOW Setting	Special Instructions
BACON **Joints**	per 500 g (1 lb)	6-8 minutes	Slit vacuum pack. Turn over during defrosting. Stand 10 minutes.
Rashers	225 g (8 oz)	2-3 minutes	Turn pack during defrosting. Stand 5 minutes.
Steaks	2 × 125 g (4 oz)	3-5 minutes	Separate during defrosting. Stand 5 minutes.
BREAD **Loaf**	large small	6-8 minutes 4-6 minutes	Wrap in kitchen paper. Turn during defrosting. Stand 5-10 minutes.
Rolls	2	15-20 seconds	Place on kitchen paper. Stand 2-3 minutes.
Slice	1 × 25 g (1 oz)	10-15 seconds	Place on kitchen paper.
CAKES **Black Forest Gâteau**	397 g (14 oz)	1½-2 minutes	Stand 30-45 minutes.
Eclairs	4	1-1½ minutes	Remove from packaging. Place on kitchen paper. Stand 15 minutes.
Mince pies, cooked	4	1-1¼ minutes	Place on kitchen paper.
FISH **Fillets, cutlets, steaks**	250 g (8 oz) 500 g (1 lb)	3-4 minutes 5-8 minutes	Separate during defrosting. Stand 5-10 minutes.
Kippers	500 g (1 lb)	4-6 minutes	Separate during defrosting. Stand 5 minutes.
Prawns	250 g (8 oz) 500 g (1 lb)	3-5 minutes 5-8 minutes	Slit pouch. Flex during defrosting. Stand 5 minutes.
Rainbow trout	200 g (7 oz)	3½ minutes	Slit pack and place on plate. Stand 5 minutes.
Whole large fish	per 500 g (1 lb)	6-8 minutes	Turn during defrosting. Stand 5-10 minutes.
MEAT **Beef – joints**	per 500 g (1 lb)	8-10 minutes	Turn over during defrosting. Stand 1 hour.
mince	500 g (1 lb)	7-10 minutes	Break up during defrosting. Stand 5-10 minutes.
steak, cubed	500 g (1 lb)	7-10 minutes	Separate during defrosting. Stand 5-10 minutes.

Food	Quantity or Weight	Time on LOW Setting	Special Instructions
Lamb/veal – chops	2 × 125 g (4 oz)	4–5 minutes	Separate during defrosting. Stand 5 minutes.
joints	per 500 g (1 lb)	6–8 minutes	Turn during defrosting. Stand 40–50 minutes.
liver, kidney	500 g (1 lb)	8–10 minutes	If sliced, separate during defrosting. Stand 5 minutes.
Pork – chops	2 × 250 g (8 oz)	6–8 minutes	Separate during defrosting. Stand 10 minutes.
joints	per 500 g (1 lb)	8–10 minutes	Turn over during defrosting. Stand 1 hour.
sausages	500 g (1 lb)	6–7 minutes	Separate during defrosting. Stand 10 minutes.
POULTRY **Chicken –** portions	2 × 250 g (8 oz)	7–9 minutes	Turn over during defrosting. Stand 10 minutes.
Chicken/ Duckling – whole	per 500 g (1 lb)	6–8 minutes	Turn over during defrosting. Stand in cold water 30 minutes. Remove giblets.
MISCELLANEOUS **Butter**	250 g (8 oz)	1½–2 minutes	Remove wrapper. Place on a plate. Stand 5 minutes.
Fruit	250 g (8 oz) 500 g (1 lb)	3–5 minutes 5–8 minutes	Stir gently during defrosting. Stand to thaw completely.
Mousse	individual	30 seconds	Remove lid. Stand 15–20 minutes.

Guide to Heating Liquids

Liquid	Amount	Approx Time on HIGH Setting
BEVERAGES Cold milk or water for instant tea, coffee, cocoa or Bovril	1 cup or mug 2 cups or mugs 4 cups or mugs	1¾–2½ minutes 3–4½ minutes 5–8 minutes
Reheating room temperature coffee	1 cup or mug 2 cups or mugs 4 cups or mugs	1½–2 minutes 3–3½ minutes 7–8 minutes
SOUP	1 individual bowl 600 ml (1 pint)	2–3 minutes 6–8 minutes

Fish, Meat and Poultry Cooking Guide

Food (fresh or defrosted)	Quantity or Weight	Time on HIGH Setting	Special Instructions
FISH **Fillets, cutlets, steaks**	500 g (1 lb)	4-5 minutes	Cook covered. Stand 5-10 minutes.
Kipper fillets	250 g (8 oz)	3 minutes	Cook covered. Stand 5 minutes.
Rainbow trout	2 × 200 g (7 oz)	6-8 minutes	Cook covered. Stand 5-10 minutes
Whole fish	1 kg (2 lb)	10-12 minutes	Cook covered. Turn over during cooking. Stand 10 minutes.
MEAT **Beef – joints**	per 500 g (1 lb)	rare: 4-6 minutes medium: 5-7 minutes well done: 6-8 minutes	Turn over during cooking. Stand 10 minutes covered with foil.
mince	500 g (1 lb)	5-6 minutes	Cook covered. Stir during cooking. Stand 2 minutes.
Lamb/veal – joints	per 500 g (1 lb)	7-9 minutes	Turn over during cooking. Stand 10 minutes covered with foil.
liver, kidneys	500 g (1 lb)	4-5 minutes	Cook covered, rearrange during cooking. Stand 5 minutes.
Pork: joints	per 500 g (1 lb)	7-9 minutes	Turn during cooking. Stand 10 minutes covered with foil.
POULTRY **Chicken – whole**	per 500 g (1 lb)	6-8 minutes	Turn over during cooking. Stand 10 minutes covered with foil.
portions	2 × 250 g (8 oz)	8-10 minutes	Cook covered. Turn over during cooking. Stand 5 minutes.
Duckling	per 500 g (1 lb)	6-8 minutes	Turn during cooking. Stand 10 minutes covered with foil.
Turkey	per 500 g (1 lb)	6-8 minutes	Turn 3-4 times during cooking. Stand 10 minutes covered with foil.

Frozen Vegetable Cooking Guide

Place vegetables with 2 tablespoons water in a dish; cover. Frozen peas and vegetables purchased in 250 g (8 oz) plastic pouches can be cooked in the slit pouch.

Vegetable	Quantity or Weight	Time on HIGH Setting	Special Instructions
Asparagus spears	250 g (8 oz)	6-7 minutes	Separate spears during cooking. Stand 2 minutes before serving.
Beans: broad	250 g (8 oz)	7-8 minutes	Stir or shake during cooking. Stand 3 minutes before serving.
green, sliced or whole	250 g (8 oz) 500 g (1 lb)	6-8 minutes 10-12 minutes	Stir during cooking. Stand 2-3 minutes before serving.
Broccoli spears	250 g (8 oz)	7-9 minutes	Rearrange spears during cooking. Stand 2-3 minutes before serving.
Brussels sprouts	250 g (8 oz)	6-7 minutes	Stir during cooking. Stand 2 minutes before serving.
Carrots	250 g (8 oz)	6-8 minutes	Stir during cooking. Stand 3 minutes before serving.
Cauliflower florets	250 g (8 oz)	7-8 minutes	Separate during cooking. Stand 2 minutes before serving.
Corn-on-the-cob	2 ears	6-7 minutes	Wrap in buttered greaseproof paper. Turn over during cooking.
Mixed vegetables, diced	250 g (8 oz) 500 g (1 lb)	4½-5½ minutes 7-9 minutes	Cook in slit pouch. Shake during cooking. Stand 2 minutes before serving. Stir during cooking. Stand 3 minutes before serving.
Peas	250 g (8 oz)	4½-5½ minutes	Cook in slit pouch. Shake during cooking. Stand 2 minutes before serving.
Stew pack	500 g (1 lb)	9-11 minutes	Stir during cooking. Stand 3 minutes before serving.
Sweetcorn	250 g (8 oz)	3-5 minutes	Stir during cooking. Stand 2 minutes before serving.

Fresh Vegetable Cooking Guide

Prepare vegetables in the usual way. Place in a dish with 2 tablespoons salted water, unless otherwise stated; cover. Prick the skin of whole vegetables, e.g. potatoes, before cooking.

Vegetable	Quantity or Weight	Time on HIGH Setting	Special Instructions
Artichokes	4 medium	15-16 minutes	Rearrange during cooking. Stand 2 minutes before serving.
Asparagus spears	500 g (1 lb)	7-9 minutes	Arrange stalks towards outside of dish. Stand 3 minutes before serving.
Aubergines	500 g (1 lb)	6-8 minutes	Stir during cooking. Stand 3 minutes before serving.
Beans broad, shelled	500 g (1 lb)	7-10 minutes	Stir during cooking. Stand 3 minutes before serving.
runner, sliced	500 g (1 lb)	8-10 minutes	Stir during cooking. Stand 2-3 minutes before serving.
Beetroot	500 g (1 lb)	7-8 minutes	Peel and slice. Do not add water. Stand 2 minutes before serving.
Broccoli spears	500 g (1 lb)	8-10 minutes	Place stems towards outside of dish. Rearrange during cooking.
Brussels sprouts	500 g (1 lb)	8-9 minutes	Stir during cooking. Stand 2-3 minutes before serving.
Cabbage, shredded	500 g (1 lb)	8-10 minutes	Stir during cooking. Stand 2-3 minutes before serving.
Carrots, sliced	250 g (8 oz)	8-9 minutes	Stir during cooking. Stand 2-3 minutes before serving.
	500 g (1 lb)	11-12 minutes	
Cauliflower florets	500 g (1 lb)	9-11 minutes	Stir during cooking. Stand 2-3 minutes before serving.
Celery, sliced	375 g (12 oz)	9-11 minutes	Stir during cooking. Stand 3 minutes before serving.
Corn-on-the-cob	2	6-8 minutes	Wrap individually in buttered greaseproof paper. Rearrange during cooking.
Courgettes, sliced	500 g (1 lb)	8-9 minutes	Do not add water. Stir during cooking.
Leeks, sliced	500 g (1 lb)	7-10 minutes	Stir during cooking. Stand 2-3 minutes before serving.

Vegetable	Quantity or Weight	Time on HIGH Setting	Special Instructions
Mushrooms	250 g (8 oz)	3-5 minutes	Do not add water. Cook in 25 g (1 oz) butter if liked. Stir during cooking.
Onions, sliced	250 g (8 oz)	5-7 minutes	Stir during cooking.
Parsnips, sliced	500 g (1 lb)	8-9 minutes	Stir during cooking. Stand 2 minutes before serving.
Peas	250 g (8 oz)	6-8 minutes	Stir during cooking. Stand 2 minutes before serving.
Potatoes, boiled	500 g (1 lb)	8-10 minutes	Cut into even-sized pieces. Stir during cooking.
jacket	2 × 250 g (8 oz)	9-10 minutes	Prick skin. Place on kitchen paper. Turn over during cooking. Stand 3-5 minutes before serving.
Spinach	500 g (1 lb)	7-9 minutes	Do not add water. Stir during cooking.
Swede/Turnip	500 g (1 lb)	8-10 minutes	Peel and dice. Stir during cooking. Time will vary with age.

Rice and Pasta Cooking Guide

Food	Weight	Time on HIGH (Standing Time)	Preparation
American, long-grain or patna rice	250 g (8 oz)	10-12 minutes (5 minutes)	Place with 600 ml (1 pint) boiling salted water and 1 tablespoon oil in a large bowl; cover.
Brown rice	250 g (8 oz)	20-25 minutes (5 minutes)	
Macaroni	250 g (8 oz)	10-12 minutes (3 minutes)	
Pasta shells, shapes	250 g (8 oz)	12-15 minutes (3 minutes)	Place with 900 ml (1½ pints) boiling salted water and 1 tablespoon oil in a large bowl; cover.
Spaghetti	250 g (8 oz)	12-15 minutes (3 minutes)	

SOUPS AND STARTERS

TOMATO SOUP

12 tomatoes, quartered
2 onions, chopped
2 celery sticks, finely
  chopped
900 ml (1½ pints)
  chicken stock
2 tablespoons tomato
  purée
2 teaspoons dried basil or
  oregano
salt and pepper
TO SERVE:
120 ml (4 fl oz) natural
  yogurt or whipping
  cream

Place the tomatoes, onion and celery in a large casserole. Add the stock, tomato purée, basil or oregano, and pepper to taste. Cook, uncovered, on HIGH for 25 minutes. Add salt to taste.

Sieve or work the soup in an electric blender or food processor, then sieve to remove skins and seeds. Swirl spoonfuls of yogurt into the soup or stir in whipping cream just before serving.

Serves 6

FRENCH ONION SOUP

500 g (1 lb) onions,
  thinly sliced
50 g (2 oz) butter or
  margarine
salt and pepper
150 ml (¼ pint) white
  wine
600 ml (1 pint) boiling
  beef stock
¼ teaspoon dried oregano
6 slices French bread,
  toasted and buttered
125 g (4 oz) Cheddar
  cheese, grated
cayenne pepper (optional)

Place the onions, butter or margarine, and salt and pepper to taste in a large bowl, cover and cook on HIGH for 6 to 7 minutes. Divide the onions between 6 soup bowls.

Mix the wine and stock together, add the oregano and pour over the onions. Cover the bowls and cook on HIGH for 10 to 12 minutes.

Place a slice of toast in each bowl, buttered side up, and sprinkle with cheese. Either place under a conventional grill until golden, or place in the microwave oven for 2 to 3 minutes, until melted.

Sprinkle with cayenne pepper, if liked, to serve.

Serves 6

MUSHROOM SOUP

25 g (1 oz) butter
1 onion, finely chopped
2 cloves garlic, crushed
  (optional)
1 litre (1¾ pints) boiling
  chicken stock or water
500 g (1 lb) mushrooms,
  thinly sliced
1 teaspoon dried mixed
  herbs
salt and pepper
2-3 tablespoons single
  cream
chopped parsley to garnish

Melt the butter in a large casserole on HIGH for 30 seconds. Add the onion and garlic, if using, and cook on HIGH for 2 to 3 minutes. Stir in the boiling stock or water, mushrooms, herbs, and salt and pepper to taste. Cover and cook on HIGH for 5 to 6 minutes or until the mushrooms are tender.

Purée in an electric blender or food processor until smooth. Reheat on HIGH for 2 to 3 minutes, if necessary.

Stir in the cream and sprinkle with chopped parsley just before serving.
Serves 6
NOTE: If a thicker soup is preferred, stir in 2 tablespoons plain flour before adding the stock.

MAIN COURSE CHICKEN SOUP

1 × 1.25-1.5 kg (2½-
    3 lb) chicken, cut into
    serving pieces
900 ml (1½ pints) water
1 onion, chopped
1 large carrot, diced
2 chicken stock cubes
50 g (2 oz) frozen peas
1 tablespoon chopped
    parsley
salt and pepper

Place the chicken and half the water in a large casserole. Stir in the onion and carrot. Cover and cook on HIGH for 30 minutes.

Remove the chicken and leave until cool. Remove the skin and bones and cut the meat into small pieces; set aside.

Skim the fat from the surface of the stock in the casserole and discard. Add the remaining water to the stock, then stir in the stock cubes, peas and parsley. Cover and cook on HIGH for 4 minutes.

Stir in the chicken, season with salt and pepper to taste, cover and cook on HIGH for 2 to 3 minutes to heat through.

Serve with garlic bread (see page 26) or hot crusty bread.
Serves 4

POTATO AND WATERCRESS SOUP

25 g (1 oz) butter
1 onion, finely chopped
1 bunch of watercress,
    finely chopped
500 g (1 lb) potatoes,
    diced
600 ml (1 pint) chicken
    stock
salt and pepper
120 ml (4 fl oz) single
    cream
TO SERVE:
garlic bread (see below)

Melt the butter in a large casserole on HIGH for 30 seconds. Add the onion, cover and cook on HIGH for 1½ minutes.

Add the watercress, potatoes, stock, and salt and pepper to taste Cover and cook on HIGH for about 15 minutes or until the vegetables are cooked.

Sieve or work in an electric blender or food processor until smooth. Return to the casserole.

Stir in the cream and cook on LOW for 3 to 4 minutes or until heated through; do not allow to boil.

Pour into a tureen. Serve hot or cold, with garlic bread.
Serves 4

GARLIC BREAD

1 small crusty French loaf
125 g (4 oz) butter
3 cloves garlic, crushed
1 teaspoon chopped
    parsley

Cut the loaf into thick slices, without cutting right through to the base of the loaf.

Mix the butter with the garlic and parsley until soft and creamy. Spread generously between the slices.

Wrap loosely in kitchen paper and heat on HIGH for 1 to 1½ minutes, until the butter has melted.

Serve with any of the soups in this chapter.
Serves 4

POTATO AND BLUE CHEESE SALAD

500 g (1 lb) new potatoes
2 tablespoons water
375 g (12 oz) tomatoes,
    chopped
6 spring onions, chopped
3 tablespoons blue cheese
    dressing
spring onions to garnish

Prick the potato skins with a fork. Place in a casserole dish with the water, cover and cook on HIGH for 10 to 12 minutes, until tender. Drain, cut into large pieces while still warm and place in a salad bowl.

Add the tomatoes, spring onions and blue cheese dressing and toss well. Chill until required. Serve, garnished with spring onions, as a starter or accompaniment.
Serves 4 to 6

LIVER PÂTÉ

250 g (8 oz) lambs' liver
2 tablespoons red wine
¼ teaspoon ground mixed
spice
½ teaspoon dried sage
1 teaspoon lemon juice
salt and pepper
125 g (4 oz) butter
2 tablespoons brandy
gherkin fans and juniper
berries to garnish

Skin the liver, cut away any membranes and cut into bite-sized pieces.

Place the wine in a casserole and heat on HIGH for 30 to 45 seconds. Add the spice, sage, lemon juice, liver, and salt and pepper to taste. Cover and cook on HIGH for 4 to 5 minutes, stirring occasionally, until the liver is cooked.

Turn the mixture into an electric blender or food processor, add the butter and brandy and work until smooth.

Pour into small individual dishes or ramekins and refrigerate overnight.

Garnish with gherkin fans and juniper berries and serve with melba toast or French bread.
Serves 4

HOT TIPSY GRAPEFRUIT

2 grapefruit
4 tablespoons rum, sherry
   or kirsch
50 g (2 oz) brown sugar
2 maraschino cherries,
   halved

Cut the grapefruit in half and loosen the segments with a grapefruit or serrated knife. Pour 1 tablespoon rum, sherry or kirsch over each half and place in individual dishes. Sprinkle the tops with sugar.

Arrange the grapefruit in their dishes in a circle in the oven and cook on HIGH for about 2 to 2½ minutes or until hot; rotate the dishes after 1½ minutes if the oven does not have a turntable.

Leave to cool for 2 minutes before serving. Decorate each one with half a maraschino cherry.
Serves 4

FISH

FISH FILLETS WITH ALMONDS

50 g (2 oz) butter
25 g (1 oz) flaked
  almonds
500 g (1 lb) white fish
  fillets
pinch of dried thyme
pinch of onion salt
2 teaspoons lemon juice
thyme sprigs

Place the butter and almonds in a dish and cook on HIGH for about 5 minutes or until the almonds are golden, stirring occasionally. Remove with a slotted spoon and set aside.

Arrange the fish in the dish with the thickest parts towards the outside. Turn to coat in the butter. Add the thyme, onion salt and lemon juice.

Cover and cook on HIGH for 5 to 6 minutes or until the fish flakes easily.

Sprinkle with the almonds and garnish with thyme sprigs. Serve with piped creamed potatoes and courgettes or peas.
Serves 4

MARINATED FISH FILLETS

500 g (1 lb) white fish
  fillets
120 ml (4 fl oz) French
  dressing
TO GARNISH:
chopped parsley
lemon wedges

Arrange the fish in a 25 × 20 cm (10 × 8 inch) dish. Pour over the French dressing and turn the fish to coat in the dressing. Cover and leave to marinate in the refrigerator for at least 2 hours.

Drain the fish fillets and rearrange them in the dish with the thickest parts towards the outside. Cover and cook on HIGH for 4 to 5 minutes or until the fish flakes easily. Leave to stand, covered, for 2 minutes.

Garnish with parsley sprigs and lemon twists. Serve with new potatoes and green beans.

Serves 4

NOTE: Sole and plaice fillets are ideal for this recipe.

SARDINE AND TOMATO QUICHE

1 × 18 cm (7 inch) pre-
  baked pastry case
2 tomatoes, sliced
2 × 120 g (4¼ oz) cans
  sardines in oil, drained
1 egg
150 ml (¼ pint) warmed
  milk
salt and pepper
TO GARNISH:
tomato slices
watercress sprigs

Place the pastry case on a flat plate
and cover the base with the tomato
slices. Arrange the sardines on top.

Beat the egg in a small bowl, stir in
the milk, and season with salt and
pepper to taste. Pour over the fish.

Cook on LOW for 12 to 15
minutes or until the centre is just set;
rotate the dish during cooking if the
oven does not have a turntable. Leave
to stand for 5 minutes.

Garnish with tomato slices and
watercress sprigs. Serve hot or cold
with salad.
Serves 4

SMOKED HADDOCK WITH PRAWN SAUCE

2 × 150 g (6 oz) packs
  frozen smoked haddock
25 g (1 oz) butter
25 g (1 oz) flour
300 ml (½ pint) milk
salt and pepper
125 g (4 oz) peeled
  prawns

Cut a small slit in the bags of smoked
haddock and place on a plate. Cook
on HIGH for 9 to 10 minutes or until
the fish is cooked; rotate the plate
after 5 minutes if the oven does not
have a turntable. Leave the fish to
stand in the bags while making the
sauce.

Place the butter in a jug in the oven
on HIGH for 1 to 1½ minutes until
melted. Blend in the flour and
gradually stir in the milk. Season
with salt and pepper to taste and cook
on HIGH for 2 minutes, stirring after
1 minute. Stir in the prawns and cook
on HIGH for 3 to 4 minutes, stirring
every minute.

Place the fish on individual
warmed serving plates and pour over
the prawn sauce. Serve with green
beans and croquette potatoes.
Serves 2

COD STEAKS NIÇOISE

1 tablespoon vegetable oil
1 onion, chopped
1 clove garlic, crushed
1 tablespoon chopped
  parsley
1 × 227 g (8 oz) can
  tomatoes, drained and
  chopped
150 ml (¼ pint) dry
  white wine
salt and pepper
2 × 250 g (8 oz) cod
  steaks
TO GARNISH:
2 black olives
parsley sprigs

Place the oil, onion and garlic in a bowl. Cover and cook on HIGH for 1½ minutes. Stir in the parsley, tomatoes, wine, and salt and pepper to taste. Cover and cook on HIGH for 2 minutes.

Arrange the cod steaks in a serving dish and pour over the sauce. Cover and cook on HIGH for 6 minutes. Leave to stand for 2 to 3 minutes.

Place a black olive in the centre of each steak and garnish with parsley sprigs. Serve with boiled new potatoes and broccoli.

Serves 2

NOTE: Fish is particularly good cooked in the microwave oven, because its texture and flavour are well retained.

STUFFED RAINBOW TROUT

4 frozen rainbow trout,
    thawed
garlic salt
1 green pepper, cored,
    seeded and sliced
1 onion, sliced
2 tomatoes, sliced
75 g (3 oz) peeled prawns
TO GARNISH:
25 g (1 oz) flaked
    almonds, toasted
watercress sprigs
lemon wedges

Wipe the trout inside and outside
with kitchen paper. Sprinkle the
cavities with garlic salt. Mix together
the green pepper, onion, tomato and
prawns and use to stuff the trout.

Cover the tails with small pieces of
foil and arrange the fish in a dish in a
single layer. Place small circles of foil
over the eyes to prevent them
'popping' during cooking. Score the
skin to prevent bursting.

Cover and cook on HIGH for 10 to
12 minutes or until the flesh can be
easily separated with a fork; rearrange
halfway through cooking if the oven
does not have a turntable. Leave to
stand for 2 to 3 minutes.

Garnish with the toasted flaked
almonds, watercress and lemon
wedges and serve with salad.
Serves 4

SOUSED HERRINGS

4 herrings, heads removed
salt and pepper
1 onion, sliced
1 teaspoon pickling spice
1-2 bay leaves
150 ml (¼ pint) malt
    vinegar
150 ml (¼ pint) water

Clean and bone the fish and remove the fins. Sprinkle with salt and pepper and roll up from head to tail. Place close together in a dish in a single layer, with the tails upwards. Scatter the onion rings on top.

Mix the remaining ingredients together, seasoning with pepper to taste, and pour over the fish. Cover and cook on HIGH for 6 to 8 minutes, rotating the dish after 3 minutes if the oven does not have a turntable. Leave to stand until cold, then chill until required. Remove the bay leaves before serving, with brown bread and salad.

Serves 4

TUNA AND MUSHROOM PIE

25 g (1 oz) butter
125 g (4 oz) mushrooms,
   sliced
1 × 298 g (10½ oz) can
   condensed cream of
   mushroom soup
2 tablespoons single cream
2 × 198 g (7 oz) cans
   tuna fish, drained and
   flaked
3 teaspoons lemon juice
salt, and pepper
500 g (1 lb) potatoes,
   cooked and mashed

Melt the butter in a casserole on
HIGH for about 30 seconds. Stir in
the mushrooms, cover and cook on
HIGH for 1 to 1½ minutes, until soft.
Stir in the remaining ingredients,
except the mashed potato, seasoning
with salt and pepper to taste.

Cover and cook on HIGH for 3 to
4 minutes or until hot, stirring after
1½ minutes.

Level the mixture in the dish and
pipe or spread the hot mashed potato
on top. If liked, place under a
preheated conventional grill to
brown. Serve with green beans.
Serves 4

MEAT AND POULTRY

LAMB IN ONION SAUCE

50 g (2 oz) butter
1 onion, sliced
625 g (1¼ lb) boned lean
  leg of lamb, cubed
2 tablespoons plain flour
1 teaspoon wine vinegar
300 ml (½ pint) boiling
  chicken stock
1 tablespoon chopped
  rosemary
salt and pepper
rosemary sprigs to garnish

Melt the butter in a casserole on HIGH for 1 minute. Stir in the onion and cook on HIGH for 2 minutes. Stir in the lamb and cook on HIGH for 7 minutes, stirring twice.

Stir in the flour and vinegar, mixing well. Carefully stir in the chicken stock, rosemary, and salt and pepper to taste.

Cover and cook on HIGH for 10 minutes or until the lamb is cooked and the sauce has thickened, stirring occasionally. Leave to stand, covered, for 5 minutes.

Check the seasoning and garnish with rosemary sprigs. Serve with green ribbon noodles or boiled rice.
Serves 4

SWEET AND SOUR LAMB

750 g (1½ lb) boned
   shoulder of lamb, cubed
3 tablespoons oil
2 onions, sliced
1 × 227 g (8 oz) can
   pineapple pieces
40 g (1½ oz) cornflour
300 ml (½ pint) chicken
   stock
1 tablespoon vinegar
2 teaspoons soy sauce
salt and pepper
1 × 213 g (7½ oz) can
   whole button
   mushrooms, drained
3 tomatoes, skinned and
   cut into wedges
chopped parsley to garnish

Place the lamb, oil and onion in a large casserole. Cover and cook on HIGH for 8 minutes, stirring after 4 minutes. Drain off any excess fat.

Drain the pineapple and blend the juice with the cornflour. Add the stock, vinegar, soy sauce, and salt and pepper to taste and blend thoroughly. Pour into the casserole.

Cover and cook on HIGH for 5 minutes, then reduce to LOW and cook for 35 to 40 minutes or until the lamb is tender.

Stir in the pineapple, mushrooms and tomatoes. Cover and cook on LOW for about 10 minutes, until heated through. Leave to stand, covered, for 5 minutes.

Sprinkle with chopped parsley and serve with jacket potatoes.
Serves 4

LIVER, BACON AND ONIONS

4 rashers back bacon,
   derinded and cut into
   5 cm (2 inch) pieces
50 g (2 oz) plain flour
salt and pepper
500 g (1 lb) lambs' liver,
   sliced
2 onions, sliced
120 ml (4 fl oz) water
1 teaspoon dried mixed
   herbs
2 tablespoons tomato
   purée

Place the bacon in a dish, cover loosely with kitchen paper and cook on HIGH for 4 minutes.

Season the flour with salt and pepper and use to coat the liver.

Drain all but 2 tablespoons bacon fat from the dish and place the liver in the dish. Add the remaining ingredients. Cover and cook on HIGH for 5 minutes, stir and continue cooking for 5 to 7 minutes, until the liver is cooked. Leave to stand, covered, for 5 minutes.

Serve with creamed potatoes or boiled rice, and peas or mangetouts.

Serves 4

ROAST LEG OF LAMB

1 × 2 kg (4½ lb) leg of
   lamb
salt and pepper
2 garlic cloves, sliced
microwave browning
   powder
1 teaspoon cornflour,
   blended with a little
   water (optional)

Wipe the joint and rub salt into the skin. Cut small slits in the surface and insert the garlic slices. Sprinkle with microwave browning powder.

Wrap a small piece of foil around the narrow end of the joint to cover about 5 cm (2 inches). Place the joint on a *microwave roasting rack* or upturned saucer in a dish and cook on HIGH for 20 minutes.

Pour off excess juices and reserve for gravy. Remove the foil and turn the joint over. Continue cooking on HIGH for 18 to 20 minutes, until a meat thermometer inserted in the thickest part of the joint registers 82°C (180°F) and the juices run clear. Leave the joint to stand, covered with foil shiny side in, for 15 minutes.

Meanwhile, strain the meat juices into a bowl, season with salt and pepper to taste and heat on high for 1 to 2 minutes or until boiling; add the blended cornflour before heating, if a thicker gravy is preferred.

Serve with mint sauce, new potatoes, carrots and the gravy.

Serves 6

PORK AND HAM LOAF

*350 g (12 oz) minced
    pork*
*350 g (12 oz) ham,
    minced*
2 eggs, beaten
50 g (2 oz) instant oats
*175 ml (6 fl oz) chilli
    sauce*
*3 tablespoons chopped
    onion*
*3 tablespoons chopped
    green pepper*
1 teaspoon dry mustard
2 tablespoons brown sugar
*tomato slices and parsley
    sprig to garnish*

Mix together the pork, ham, eggs, oats, 4 tablespoons of the chilli sauce, the onion, green pepper and half the mustard.

Press into a 23 × 13 cm (9 × 5 inch) loaf dish, smoothing the surface and leaving about 5 mm (¼ inch) space around the edges for the juices to drain during cooking.

Cover with greaseproof paper and cook on HIGH for 5 minutes. Leave to stand for 5 minutes. Drain off juices and smooth the surface.

Mix together the sugar, and remaining chilli sauce and mustard and spread over the loaf, coating the top and sides completely.

Cover with greaseproof paper and cook on LOW for 30 to 35 minutes. Cover with foil and leave to stand for 5 minutes.

Garnish with tomato and parsley. Serve hot with vegetables, or cold with a rice salad.
Serves 6

MARINATED RABBIT

1 kg (2 lb) rabbit joints
salt and pepper
1 onion, sliced
300 ml (½ pint) dry
    white wine
300 ml (½ pint) chicken
    stock
1 bay leaf
1 level tablespoon
    cornflour, blended with
    a little water
12 cocktail silverskin
    onions
12 stuffed green olives,
    sliced
1 × 213 g (7½ oz) can
    button mushrooms,
    drained and halved
parsley sprig to garnish

Rub the rabbit joints with salt and pepper and place in a dish with the onion, wine, stock and bay leaf. Cover and leave to marinate in the refrigerator overnight.

Discard the onion and bay leaf. Place the rabbit and marinade in a casserole, cover and cook on HIGH for 15 to 20 minutes or until tender. Remove the rabbit and set aside.

Stir the blended cornflour into the casserole, cover and bring to the boil on HIGH, stirring frequently. Stir in the onions, olives and mushrooms and return the rabbit to the casserole.

Cover and cook on HIGH for 2 to 3 minutes, until heated through. Leave to stand, covered, for 5 minutes.

Garnish with parsley and serve with boiled potatoes and buttered mashed swedes.
Serves 4

CHICKEN PAPRIKA

1 × 1-1.5 kg (2-3½ lb)
  chicken, jointed into 4
  or 6 pieces
2 tablespoons oil
1 large onion, chopped
1 green pepper, cored,
  seeded and chopped
1 level tablespoon mild
  paprika
1 level tablespoon tomato
  purée
2 large tomatoes, skinned
  and chopped
150 ml (¼ pint) chicken
  stock
salt and pepper
2 tablespoons natural
  yogurt
parsley sprig to garnish

Arrange the chicken joints in a dish in a single layer, with the meatiest portions towards the outside.

Cover and cook on HIGH for 10 minutes, rotating the dish after 5 minutes if the oven does not have a turntable.

Meanwhile, heat the oil in a frying pan, add the onion and green pepper and fry conventionally until golden. Stir in the paprika, tomato purée, tomatoes, stock, and salt and pepper to taste. Bring to the boil and pour over the chicken.

Cover and cook on HIGH for about 20 minutes or until the chicken is tender. Leave to stand, covered, for 5 minutes, then stir in the yogurt.

Garnish with parsley and serve with a green salad.

Serves 4 to 6

ROAST CHICKEN

1 × 2 kg (4½ lb) oven-
  ready chicken
melted butter
microwave seasoning
  (optional)

Wipe and dry the chicken thoroughly, inside and out. Truss firmly to give a good shape, with wings and legs close to the body. Brush all over with melted butter and cover the wing and leg tips with foil.

Sprinkle with microwave seasoning, if using, and place, breast side down, on a *microwave roasting rack* or upturned saucer in a dish. Cook on HIGH for 16 minutes.

Drain off excess juices, remove the foil and turn the chicken breast side up. Continue cooking on HIGH for 16 minutes or until a meat thermometer inserted in the thickest part of each thigh registers 85°C (185°F) and the juices run clear.

Cover with a tent of foil, shiny side in, and leave to stand for 20 minutes.

Serve with bread sauce, gravy, bacon rolls and game chips.

Serves 6

CHICKEN À LA KING

50 g (2 oz) butter
2 tablespoons chopped
     green pepper
2 tablespoons chopped red
     pepper
2 tablespoons plain flour
milk
1 × 298 g (10 ½ oz) can
     condensed cream of
     chicken soup
350-500 g (12 oz-1 lb)
     cooked chicken, cubed
2 tablespoons dry white
     wine
1 × 213 g (7½ oz) can
     button mushrooms,
     drained and halved
salt and pepper
TO SERVE:
French bread, sliced and
     toasted

Place the butter and peppers in a
casserole, cover and cook on HIGH
for 2 minutes. Stir in the flour until
smooth.

Add enough milk to the soup to
make 450 ml (¾ pint) then blend into
the flour mixture.

Cook on HIGH for 5½ to 7½
minutes or until thickened, stirring
occasionally.

Stir in the remaining ingredients,
with salt and pepper to taste, and
cook on HIGH for 2½ to 3½ minutes
or until heated through.

Arrange the French bread on
warmed individual serving plates and
spoon the chicken mixture on top.
Serves 4

45

TURKEY TETRAZZINI

4 rashers streaky bacon,
  derinded
4 tablespoons oil
125 g (4 oz) mushrooms,
  sliced
1 onion, chopped
4 tablespoons plain flour
salt and pepper
350 ml (12 fl oz) boiling
  chicken stock
350 ml (12 fl oz) milk
3 tablespoons dry sherry
250 g (8 oz) spaghetti,
  cooked and drained
350 g (12 oz) cooked
  turkey, cubed
50 g (2 oz) grated
  Parmesan cheese
chopped parsley to garnish

Snip the bacon fat at regular intervals and place the rashers between a double thickness of kitchen paper on a plate. Cook on HIGH for 4 to 5 minutes or until crisp. Crumble and set aside.

Place the oil in a large casserole, add the mushrooms and onion and cook on HIGH for 4 minutes or until the onion is tender, stirring once.

Stir in the flour, and salt and pepper to taste and cook on HIGH for 30 seconds. Add the stock and milk, mix well and cook on HIGH until bubbling and thickened, stirring during cooking.

Stir in the sherry, spaghetti, turkey, bacon and cheese, mixing well. Cover and cook on HIGH for 10 to 12 minutes or until heated through, stirring once.

Stir and garnish with chopped parsley to serve.
Serves 4

ROAST DUCK

1 × 2.25 kg (5 lb) oven-
ready duckling
2 tablespoons orange jelly
marmalade
TO GARNISH:
watercress sprigs
orange twists

Wash and dry the duckling inside and out. Truss securely to give a compact shape. Prick the skin with a fork and brush all over with the marmalade.

Place breast side down on a *microwave roasting rack* or upturned saucer in a dish and cook on HIGH for 15 minutes.

Drain off juices, turn breast side up and continue cooking on HIGH for 15 to 20 minutes or until a meat thermometer inserted in the thickest part of each thigh registers 85°C (185°F) and the juices run clear.

Cover with a tent of foil, shiny side in, and leave to stand for 10 to 15 minutes. Serve garnished with watercress and orange twists.
Serves 4

TURKEY SUPREME

500 g (1 lb) frozen
asparagus spears
50 g (2 oz) butter
25 g (1 oz) flaked
almonds
1 tablespoon cornflour
1 × 298 g (10½ oz) can
condensed cream of
asparagus soup
120 ml (4 fl oz) chicken
stock
salt and pepper
750 g (1½ lb) cooked
turkey, diced
paprika
TO GARNISH:
chopped parsley
flaked almonds

Cut a small slit in the top of the asparagus bags and place in a shallow dish. Cook on HIGH for 5 minutes.

Remove the spears from the bags, place in a dish, cover and cook on HIGH for 5 minutes. Set aside.

Melt the butter in a casserole on HIGH for 30 seconds. Stir in the almonds and cook on HIGH for 1 to 1½ minutes; stir every 30 seconds.

Stir in the cornflour, soup, stock, and salt and pepper to taste, stirring well to blend. Cook on HIGH for 3 to 4 minutes, until boiling and thickened, stirring every minute.

Place alternate layers of turkey and asparagus in a 30 × 20 cm (12 × 8 inch) dish, cover with the sauce and sprinkle with paprika.

Cook on HIGH for 4 to 5 minutes or until heated through, rotating the dish every 2 minutes if the oven does not have a turntable.

Garnish with chopped parsley and flaked almonds to serve.
Serves 6

VEGETABLE DISHES

Vegetables are excellent cooked by microwave. Because they cook quickly, they retain more flavour, colour and nutrients than those cooked conventionally.

BROAD BEAN MEDLEY

2 tablespoons oil
1 clove garlic, crushed
1 onion, finely chopped
500 g (1 lb) shelled broad
  beans
350 g (12 oz) tomatoes,
  skinned and roughly
  chopped
1 teaspoon caster sugar
½ teaspoon oregano
2 tablespoons wine
  vinegar
salt and pepper

Place the oil, garlic and onion in a casserole, cover and cook on HIGH for 2 minutes. Stir in the beans, mixing well. Stir in the remaining ingredients, with salt and pepper to taste. Cover and cook on HIGH for 8 to 10 minutes or until the broad beans are tender.
Serves 4

BROCCOLI AND CAULIFLOWER CHEESE

250 g (8 oz) frozen
    broccoli spears
250 g (8 oz) frozen
    cauliflower florets
2 tablespoons water
1 packet cheese sauce mix
250 ml (8 fl oz) milk
25 g (1 oz) butter
25 g (1 oz) dried
    breadcrumbs
chopped parsley to garnish

Place the broccoli, cauliflower and water in a casserole. Cover and cook on HIGH for 10 to 12 minutes or until tender, stirring once or twice during cooking. Drain and return to the dish. Cover and set aside.

Blend the cheese sauce mix with the milk in a Pyrex measure. Cook on HIGH for about 3 minutes or until thickened, stirring every minute.

Melt the butter in a small dish on HIGH for 15 to 30 seconds and stir in the breadcrumbs.

Pour the cheese sauce over the vegetables and sprinkle with the buttered breadcrumbs. If necessary, reheat on HIGH for about 2 minutes before serving, sprinkled with chopped parsley.

Serves 4 to 6

CAULIFLOWER POLONAISE

50 g (2 oz) butter
50 g (2 oz) coarse
  breadcrumbs
1 cauliflower, broken into
  florets
2 tablespoons water
1 tablespoon finely
  chopped parsley
2 hard-boiled eggs, finely
  chopped

Melt the butter in a bowl on HIGH for 1 minute. Stir in the breadcrumbs and set aside.

Place the cauliflower and water in a casserole, cover and cook on HIGH for 8 to 10 minutes or until tender. Drain thoroughly.

Mix the buttered crumbs with the parsley and eggs and sprinkle over the cauliflower to serve.

Serves 4

PEAS BONNE FEMME

125 g (4 oz) streaky
  bacon, derinded and
  diced
25 g (1 oz) butter
500 g (1 lb) frozen peas
6 small white button
  onions
120 ml (4 fl oz) water
salt and pepper
15 g (½ oz) caster sugar
10 small lettuce leaves

Place the bacon in a casserole, cover with kitchen paper and cook on HIGH for 3 to 4 minutes.

Add the butter, peas, onions, water, and salt and pepper to taste. Cover and cook on HIGH for 8 minutes, stirring after 4 minutes.

Stir in the sugar and lettuce leaves, cover and cook on HIGH for 2 minutes or until the peas and onions are tender.

Serves 4 to 6

BAKED BEAN AND POTATO CASSEROLE

1 × 447 g (15¾ oz) can
  baked beans
1 kg (2 lb) freshly cooked
  hot potatoes, sliced
250 g (8 oz) Cheddar
  cheese, grated
salt and pepper

Spoon half the baked beans into a casserole. Cover with half the potatoes and sprinkle half the grated cheese on top. Season with salt and pepper to taste. Spoon the remaining baked beans on top and cover with the remaining potato. Cover and cook on HIGH for about 4 minutes or until heated through.

Sprinkle with the remaining cheese, cover and heat for a further 1 to 2 minutes or until the cheese has melted.

Serve as a light lunch or supper dish.

Serves 4

SUPPERS AND SNACKS

The microwave oven is ideal for preparing quick suppers and snacks. Traditional favourites can be cooked in a fraction of the normal time.

SPANISH OMELET

*125 g (4 oz) frozen
  mixed vegetables*
1 tomato, chopped
1 cooked potato, chopped
¼ red pepper, chopped
1 small onion, chopped
2 tablespoons vegetable oil
4 eggs
salt and pepper
parsley sprigs to garnish

Place the vegetables and oil in a large shallow pie plate, cover and cook on HIGH for 4 minutes.

Beat the eggs with salt and pepper to taste and pour over the vegetables. Cook on LOW for 8 to 10 minutes, until set. Do not fold the omelet. If preferred, place under a preheated conventional grill to brown the top.

Garnish with parsley sprigs and serve with a green salad.
Serves 2

MACKEREL IN GOOSEBERRY SAUCE

50 g (2 oz) butter
75 g (3 oz) fresh
   breadcrumbs
2 tablespoons chopped
   parsley
2 tablespoons finely
   chopped red pepper
1 teaspoon dried basil
2 teaspoons lemon juice
salt and pepper
2 mackerel, cleaned
1 × 283 g (10 oz) can
   gooseberries
TO GARNISH:
lemon twists
parsley sprigs

Melt the butter in a bowl on HIGH for 1 minute. Stir in the breadcrumbs, parsley, red pepper, basil, lemon juice, and salt and pepper to taste and mix well to form the stuffing.

Cut the heads and tails from the mackerel. Fill the cavities with the stuffing. Arrange in a dish and make 3 slits in the skin of each fish.

Place the gooseberries with their juice in an electric blender or food processor and work until smooth. Pour over the fish.

Cover and cook on HIGH for 7 minutes. Leave to stand for 2 to 3 minutes. Garnish with lemon twists and parsley and serve with boiled new potatoes.
Serves 2

APPLE AND BACON SUPPER

500 g (1 lb) onions, sliced
2 tablespoons water
500 g (1 lb) cooking
    apples, peeled, cored
    and sliced
pepper
375 g (12 oz) streaky
    bacon, derinded

Place the onions and water in a casserole, cover and cook on HIGH for 8 minutes or until tender.

Stir in the apple slices and pepper to taste. Cover and cook on HIGH for 3 minutes, stirring once. Set aside.

Meanwhile, place the bacon on a *microwave roasting rack*, or between layers of kitchen paper, in a dish and cook on HIGH for 5 to 6 minutes, pouring off excess fat after every 2 minutes.

Crumble the bacon and stir into the onion and apple mixture. Cover and cook on HIGH for 2 minutes or until heated through.

Serve with hot crusty bread.
Serves 4

SPICY DRUMSTICKS

8 chicken drumsticks
1 sachet seasoned coating
    mix for chicken, any
    flavour

Skin the drumsticks and coat with the seasoning following packet instructions. Arrange in a single layer in a dish with the thicker ends towards the outside of the dish. Cover and cook on HIGH for 4 minutes.

Turn the drumsticks over, cover and cook on HIGH for 4 minutes. Uncover and leave to stand for a few minutes.

Serve on their own or with salad.
Serves 4

WELSH RAREBIT

4 tablespoons beer
1 teaspoon dry mustard
dash of cayenne
1 teaspoon Worcestershire
    sauce
250 g (8 oz) matured
    Cheddar cheese, grated
4 slices toast to serve

Combine the beer, mustard, cayenne and Worcestershire sauce in a bowl.

Stir in the cheese and cook on LOW for about 3 minutes or until melted, stirring twice.

Stir and serve immediately on the toast.
Serves 4

HAM AND VEGETABLE PILAU

250 g (8 oz) carrots, thinly sliced

250 g (8 oz) cauliflower florets

125 g (4 oz) leeks, thinly sliced

25 g (1 oz) butter

250 g (8 oz) long-grain rice

1/2 teaspoon each ground cardamom, paprika and ground cinnamon

1/2 teaspoon turmeric (optional)

600 ml (1 pint) chicken stock

125 g (4 oz) cooked ham, cut into strips

1 tablespoon chopped parsley

Place the vegetables and butter in a casserole, cover and cook on HIGH for 5 minutes. Add the rice, spices and stock, cover and cook on HIGH for 7 to 8 minutes.

Reduce the setting to LOW and cook for 15 minutes, stirring occasionally. Stir in the ham and cook on HIGH for 2 to 3 minutes to heat through.

Sprinkle with the parsley to serve.

Serves 4

SPAGHETTI BOLOGNESE

500 g (1 lb) minced beef
1 onion, chopped
3 tablespoons chopped
    green pepper
1 × 397 g (14 oz) can
    tomatoes, drained and
    cut into large pieces
2 tablespoons tomato
    purée
1 × 150 g (5 oz) can
    tomato paste
4 tablespoons water
1 bay leaf
2 teaspoons dried oregano
1 teaspoon dried basil
1 tablespoon
    Worcestershire sauce
175 g (12 oz) spaghetti
salt
1 tablespoon oil
grated Parmesan cheese to
    serve

Place the minced beef, onion and green pepper in a casserole, stirring to break up the beef. Cover with greaseproof paper and cook on HIGH for 5 to 6 minutes, stirring twice. Pour off excess juices.

Stir in the tomatoes, tomato purée, tomato paste, water, bay leaf, oregano, basil and Worcestershire sauce. Cover and cook on HIGH for 10 minutes, or until boiling. Stir well, cover and cook on LOW for 20 to 25 minutes, until tender, stirring occasionally.

Meanwhile, cook the spaghetti in boiling salted water, adding the oil, on a conventional cooker for 10 to 12 minutes, until al dente. Drain and place in a warmed serving dish.

Pour over the meat sauce, discarding the bay leaf, and sprinkle with Parmesan cheese to serve.

Serves 4

DEVILLED KIDNEYS

2 tablespoons plain flour
salt and pepper
8 lambs' kidneys,
    skinned, halved and
    cored
25 g (1 oz) butter
1 small onion, chopped
1 tablespoon
    Worcestershire sauce
1 tablespoon dry sherry
1 tablespoon chopped
    parsley
TO SERVE:
2-3 rounds of fried bread,
    or croûtons
parsley sprig

Season the flour with salt and pepper and use to coat the kidneys.

Melt the butter in a shallow dish on HIGH for 1 minute. Add the onion, cover and cook on HIGH for 1½ minutes. Stir in the kidneys, cover and cook on HIGH for 4 minutes, stirring after 2 minutes.

Stir in the Worcestershire sauce, sherry and parsley, cover and cook on HIGH for 2 to 3 minutes. Leave to stand for 5 minutes. Serve, garnished with parsley, on rounds of fried bread, or with croûtons.

Serves 2

CHILLI CON CARNE

500 g (1 lb) minced beef
1 onion, chopped
2 tablespoons chopped
   green pepper
1 × 397 g (14 oz) can
   tomatoes
2 tablespoons tomato
   purée
1 teaspoon dried oregano
1 large bay leaf
1 teaspoon chilli powder
salt
1 × 425 g (15 oz) can red
   kidney beans, drained
   and rinsed
grated cheese to serve

Place the minced beef, onion and green pepper in a casserole, stirring to break up the meat. Cover with greaseproof paper and cook on HIGH for 5 minutes or until browned, stirring twice. Pour off excess juices.

Stir in the tomatoes with their juice, tomato purée, oregano, bay leaf, chilli powder, and salt to taste, mixing well. Gently stir in the beans.

Cover and cook on HIGH for 7 minutes or until boiling. Stir well, cover and cook on LOW for 20 to 30 minutes, until tender, stirring occasionally. Remove the bay leaf.

Spoon into individual warmed bowls and sprinkle with grated cheese. Serve with warm crusty bread.
Serves 4

BEEFBURGERS

500 g (1 lb) minced beef
1 onion, minced or grated
½ teaspoon dried mixed
  herbs
1 teaspoon chopped
  parsley
salt and pepper
Worcestershire sauce
TO SERVE:
4 sesame seed baps
burger mustard or tomato
  relish
tomato slices
few lettuce leaves
onion rings

Mix together the minced beef, onion, herbs, and salt and pepper to taste. Shape into 4 thick, flat rounds. Place in a circle on a plate, brush the tops with Worcestershire sauce, and cook on HIGH for 3 minutes. Pour off excess juices.

Turn the beefburgers over, brush with Worcestershire sauce and cook on HIGH for 3 to 4 minutes or until cooked according to taste.

Place the beefburgers in the baps, spread with mustard or relish and top with tomato slices.

Arrange in a circle on kitchen paper in the oven and heat on HIGH for 45 to 60 seconds; do not overheat or the baps will toughen.

Garnish with lettuce and onion rings to serve.
Serves 4

VEGETARIAN QUICHE

75 g (3 oz) mushrooms, sliced
25 g (1 oz) butter
25 g (1 oz) plain flour
300 ml (½ pint) milk
1 teaspoon mixed herbs
salt and pepper
1 egg
250 g (8 oz) mixed vegetables, cooked
75 g (3 oz) matured Cheddar cheese, grated
1 × 18 cm (7 inch) pre-baked pastry flan case
parsley sprig to garnish

Place the mushrooms and butter in a dish, cover and cook on HIGH for 3 minutes.

Blend together the flour, milk, herbs, and salt and pepper to taste in a basin. Cook on HIGH for 4 minutes, stirring every minute. Beat in the egg, then stir in the vegetables and 50 g (2 oz) of the cheese.

Turn the mixture into the flan case and sprinkle the remaining cheese on top. Stand the quiche on a piece of kitchen paper, placed on a plate. Cook on LOW for about 15 minutes or until the filling is set; rotate the quiche during cooking if the oven does not have a turntable.

Garnish with parsley and serve warm or cold with a green salad.
Serves 4

MOCK LASAGNE

227 g (8 oz) frozen
  chopped spinach
500 g (1 lb) minced beef
1 teaspoon garlic salt
1 × 397 g (14 oz) can
  tomatoes, liquidized or
  sieved
4 tablespoons dried
  breadcrumbs
227 g (8 oz) cottage
  cheese
1 egg, beaten
pepper
125 g (4 oz) Mozzarella
  cheese, sliced
2 tablespoons grated
  Parmesan cheese

Remove the spinach from its wrapper and place in a small dish. Cover and cook on HIGH for 3 minutes or until defrosted. Drain well and set aside.

Place the minced beef in a casserole, stirring to break it up, and sprinkle with the garlic salt. Cook on HIGH for 5 to 6 minutes or until browned, stirring after 2 minutes. Drain off excess juices. Stir in the tomatoes, cover and cook on HIGH for about 1 minute, until bubbling. Stir in half the breadcrumbs.

Place the spinach, cottage cheese, egg, remaining breadcrumbs, and pepper to taste in a bowl; mix well.

Spread half the meat mixture in a 23 cm (9 inch) square dish. Cover with the spinach mixture then the Mozzarella cheese. Top with the remaining meat and sprinkle with the Parmesan cheese.

Cook on HIGH for 4 minutes, rotate the dish if the oven does not have a turntable, and cook on HIGH for a further 4 minutes. Leave to stand for 5 minutes before serving.
Serves 4

SAUSAGE PATTIES WITH BEANS

250 g (8 oz) sausagemeat
1 × 219 g (7¾ oz) can
  baked beans

Divide the sausagemeat into 4 equal pieces and form into round patties about 7.5 cm (3 inches) in diameter.

Preheat a *microwave browning dish* according to manufacturer's instructions. Place the patties in the dish, pressing down well with a palette knife to make maximum contact with the hot surface. Cook on HIGH for 1½ minutes, turn over and cook for 1½ to 2 minutes or until browned and tender.

Place the beans in a dish, cover and cook on HIGH for 1½ minutes.

Serve with the patties.
Serves 2

BAKING AND DESSERTS

VICTORIA SANDWICH CAKE

*125 g (4 oz) soft
   margarine*
125 g (4 oz) caster sugar
*125 g (4 oz) self-raising
   flour, sifted*
1 teaspoon baking powder
2 eggs, beaten
2 tablespoons warm water
TO FINISH:
*3 tablespoons raspberry or
   strawberry jam*
*120 ml (4 fl oz) double
   cream, whipped
   (optional)*
icing sugar, sifted

Place all the cake ingredients in a
bowl and beat together until smooth
and creamy. Turn into a greased
18 cm (7 inch) soufflé dish and level
the top.

Cook on HIGH for 4 to 4½
minutes, rotating the dish after
2 minutes if the oven does not have
a turntable. Leave to stand for
5 minutes, then turn onto a wire rack
to cool.

Cut the cake in half horizontally
and sandwich together with the jam,
and cream if using. Sprinkle the top
with icing sugar before serving.
Makes one 18 cm (7 inch) cake

NUT AND BANANA TEABREAD

125 g (4 oz) margarine
125 g (4 oz) soft dark
 brown sugar
2 eggs, beaten
1 banana, mashed
1 teaspoon lemon juice
175 g (6 oz) self-raising
 flour, sifted
½ teaspoon bicarbonate of
 soda
50 g (2 oz) chopped
 mixed nuts
50 g (2 oz) Brazil nuts
14 glacé cherries
clear honey to glaze

Cream the margarine and sugar together until light and fluffy. Beat in the eggs, banana and lemon juice, then fold in the flour, bicarbonate of soda and nuts.

Pour into a greased 23 × 13 × 7.5 cm (9 × 5 × 3 inch) loaf-shaped dish. Place the dish on an upturned plate in the oven and cook on HIGH for 7 to 8 minutes, until cooked in the centre. Turn the dish every 2 minutes if the oven does not have a turntable.

Leave to stand for 5 minutes, then turn onto a wire rack. Arrange the nuts and cherries over the top and brush with honey. Leave to cool. Serve sliced, with butter.

Makes 1 loaf

CHOCOLATE RUM GÂTEAU

1 tablespoon cocoa powder
2 tablespoons boiling
  water
125 g (4 oz) soft
  margarine
125 g (4 oz) caster sugar
125 g (4 oz) self-raising
  flour, sifted
1 teaspoon baking powder
2 eggs, beaten
CHOCOLATE SYRUP:
125 g (4 oz) granulated
  sugar
1 tablespoon cocoa powder
150 ml (¼ pint) water
2 tablespoons rum
TO DECORATE:
284 ml (10 fl oz) double
  cream
1 tablespoon milk
chocolate leaves (see
  below)

Blend the cocoa and water together until smooth; leave to cool. Place in a mixing bowl with the remaining cake ingredients and beat until smooth.

Spoon into a 23 cm (9 inch) microwave ring mould and level the top. Cook on HIGH for 4 to 5 minutes. Leave to stand for 10 minutes, then turn onto a wire rack to cool.

Meanwhile, make the syrup. Place the sugar, cocoa and water in a bowl and cook on HIGH for 1½ to 2 minutes, until dissolved. Cool and stir in the rum.

Return the cake to the ring mould, pour over the syrup and leave to soak for 10 to 15 minutes.

Whip the cream and milk together. Place the cake on a serving plate, cover with the cream and decorate with chocolate leaves.

Serves 6 to 8

CHOCOLATE LEAVES: Coat the underside of fresh clean leaves with melted chocolate, using a fine paint brush. Leave to set, chocolate side up, then carefully peel the leaf away.

MADELEINES

125 g (4 oz) soft
  margarine
125 g (4 oz) caster sugar
2 eggs, beaten
125 g (4 oz) self-raising
  flour, sifted
6 tablespoons raspberry
  jam
desiccated coconut to cover
6 glacé cherry halves to
  decorate

Place the margarine, sugar, eggs and flour in a bowl and beat together until light and fluffy. Divide equally between 6 paper drinking cups.

Arrange in a circle in the oven and cook on HIGH for about 3½ minutes, rearranging the cups after 1½ minutes and removing any which are cooked sooner. Flex the cups and turn onto a wire rack to cool.

Place the jam in a small bowl and heat on HIGH for 30 to 40 seconds, stirring after 15 seconds. Brush the cold cakes with warmed jam and roll in the coconut to coat. Place a glacé cherry half on top of each to decorate.

Makes 6

CHRISTMAS PUDDING

65 g (2½ oz) plain flour
1 teaspoon ground mixed
  spice
75 g (3 oz) breadcrumbs
50 g (2 oz) shredded suet
125 g (4 oz) soft dark
  brown sugar
375 g (12 oz) mixed dried
  fruit
1 small dessert apple,
  peeled and chopped
grated rind of ½ an orange
2 eggs, beaten
1 tablespoon black treacle
2 tablespoons brandy
4 tablespoons milk

Sift the flour and spice into a mixing bowl. Add the breadcrumbs, suet, sugar, dried fruit, apple and orange rind, and mix well. Add the eggs, treacle, brandy and milk and stir well to mix.

Turn into a greased 900 ml (1½ pint) pudding basin, cover and cook on HIGH for 8 to 10 minutes. Leave to stand for 5 to 10 minutes before turning out.

Serve with brandy butter or whipped cream.

Serves 4 to 6

NOTE: This pudding can be cooked in advance and left to mature. Wrap in greaseproof paper and foil and store in a cool dry place. When required, unwrap, replace in the pudding basin, cover and reheat on HIGH for about 2 minutes; do not overheat. Leave to stand for 2 minutes before serving.

COFFEE MARBLE CROWN

125 g (4 oz) self-raising
    flour
125 g (4 oz) soft
    margarine
125 g (4 oz) caster sugar
2 eggs, beaten
1 tablespoon milk
3 teaspoons instant coffee
    powder or granules
120 ml (4 fl oz) warm
    water
TO FINISH:
1 kiwi fruit, sliced
1 nectarine, sliced
few strawberries, sliced
few seedless grapes
142 ml (5 fl oz) double
    cream, whipped

Sift the flour into a bowl, add the
margarine, sugar, eggs and milk and
beat well.

Turn into a 23 cm (9 inch)
microwave ring mould and cook on
HIGH for 4 minutes. Leave to stand
for 2 to 3 minutes, then turn onto a
wire rack to cool.

Mix the coffee powder or granules
with the water in a small basin and
heat on HIGH for 1 minute.

Return the cooled cake to the ring
mould and pour over the coffee.
Leave to soak for 30 minutes.

Turn out onto a serving plate and
fill the centre with the fruit. Pipe
cream around the top and side to
decorate.
Serves 6 to 8

BAKED STUFFED APPLES

4 cooking apples, cored
4 tablespoons mincemeat
4 tablespoons apple juice
  (optional)

Prick the skins of the apples with a fork and arrange in a circle on a dish.

Fill the cavities with mincemeat and drizzle with the apple juice, if using. Cover and cook on HIGH for 7 to 9 minutes, depending on size, until almost tender. Leave to stand, covered, for 5 minutes.

Spoon over the juices and serve with whipped cream.

Serves 4

JAM SPONGE PUDDING

125 g (4 oz) margarine
125 g (4 oz) caster sugar
2 eggs, beaten
125 g (4 oz) plain flour,
  sifted
1 level teaspoon baking
  powder
1 tablespoon warm water
3 tablespoons jam

Cream the margarine and sugar together until light and fluffy. Beat in the eggs, then fold in the flour, baking powder and water.

Place the jam in the base of a 900 ml (1½ pint) pudding basin and heat on HIGH for 30 seconds.

Add the sponge mixture, cover and cook on HIGH for about 6 minutes. Leave to stand for 5 minutes, before turning out to serve.

Serves 4 to 6

APRICOT CRUNCH

50 g (2 oz) butter
50 g (2 oz) soft dark
  brown sugar
50 g (2 oz) porridge oats
50 g (2 oz) plain flour,
  sifted
1 × 397 g (14 oz) can
  apricot pie filling
1 tablespoon demerara
  sugar
2 tablespoons crunchnut
  topping or mixed
  chopped nuts

Melt the butter in a bowl on HIGH for 45 to 60 seconds. Stir in the soft brown sugar and oats. Cook on HIGH for 2 minutes.

Stir in the flour, using a knife to cut into the mixture, until it resembles coarse breadcrumbs.

Place the apricot pie filling in the base of the greased 900 ml (1½ pint) pie dish and cover with the oat mixture. Sprinkle with the demerara sugar and crunchnut topping or nuts.

Cook on HIGH for 8 to 10 minutes, rotating the dish halfway during cooking if the oven does not have a turntable.

Serve warm with cream.

Serves 4

SAUCES AND PRESERVES

BARBECUE SAUCE

1 large onion, chopped
2 tablespoons oil
1 clove garlic, crushed
1 × 142 g (5 oz) can
    tomato purée
2 tablespoons lemon juice
2 tablespoons soft dark
    brown sugar
150 ml (¼ pint) beef
    stock
2 tablespoons
    Worcestershire sauce
2 teaspoons dry mustard
salt and pepper

Place the onion and oil in a large jug,
cover and cook on HIGH for
4 minutes. Blend in the remaining
ingredients, seasoning with salt and
pepper to taste. Cover and cook on
HIGH for 4 minutes, stirring once
during cooking.

Serve with sausages, chops,
kebabs, and barbecued meat and
poultry.

Makes about 450 ml (¾ pint)

TOMATO SAUCE

25 g (1 oz) butter
1 onion, chopped
1 clove garlic, finely
    chopped
1 tablespoon plain flour
1 × 397 g (14 oz) can
    tomatoes
1 teaspoon dried oregano
salt and pepper
chopped parsley to serve
    (optional)

Place the butter, onion and garlic in a bowl, cover and cook on HIGH for 3 minutes. Stir in the flour. Add the tomatoes with their juice, oregano, and salt and pepper to taste. Cover and cook on HIGH for 5 to 7 minutes, stirring twice.

Sieve or work in an electric blender or food processor if a smooth sauce is preferred.

Serve with pasta, meat, poultry and vegetables. Sprinkle with chopped parsley before serving if preferred.

Makes about 300 ml (½ pint)

BÉCHAMEL SAUCE

300 ml (½ pint) milk
½ small bay leaf
thyme sprig
¼ teaspoon grated nutmeg
25 g (1 oz) butter
25 g (1 oz) plain flour
salt and pepper

Place the milk, bay leaf, thyme and nutmeg in a dish and cook on HIGH for 2 minutes. Leave to infuse for at least 15 minutes, then strain and set aside.

Melt the butter in a jug on HIGH for 30 to 45 seconds. Stir in the flour and gradually blend in the infused milk.

Cook on HIGH for 3 to 4 minutes, until the sauce has boiled and thickened. Stir every minute.

Season with salt and pepper to taste. Use as required.

Makes 300 ml (½ pint)

VARIATIONS:
Cheese Sauce: Add 50-75 g (2-3 oz) grated matured Cheddar cheese and 1 teaspoon dry mustard to the sauce 1 minute before the end of the cooking time.
Mushroom Sauce: Add 125 g (4 oz) cooked or canned sliced mushrooms to the sauce 2 minutes before the end of the cooking time. Serve with fish.
Parsley Sauce: Add 1 tablespoon chopped parsley to the cooked sauce. Serve with fish.
Egg Sauce: Add 2 chopped hard-boiled eggs to the sauce 2 minutes before the end of the cooking time. Serve with fish.

ONION SAUCE

1 onion, chopped
25 g (1 oz) butter
25 g (1 oz) plain flour
300 ml (½ pint) milk
salt and pepper

Place the onion and butter in a bowl, cover and cook on HIGH for 4 minutes. Stir in the flour, then gradually add the milk, stirring constantly. Season with salt and pepper to taste. Cook on HIGH for 4 minutes, stirring every minute.

Serve with cooked joints of lamb or lamb chops.

Makes 300 ml (½ pint)

APPLE SAUCE

500 g (1 lb) cooking
    apples, peeled, cored
    and thinly sliced
15 g (½ oz) butter
1 tablespoon water
a few drops of lemon juice
sugar

Place the apples, butter and water in a casserole. Cover and cook on HIGH for 6 to 8 minutes, stirring after 3 minutes. Sieve, beat or work in an electric blender or food processor until smooth. Add lemon juice and sugar to taste.

Serve with roast pork, goose or duck, or as required.
Makes 200 ml (⅓ pint)

MARMALADE SAUCE

4 tablespoons marmalade
4 tablespoons water
1 tablespoon lemon juice

Place all the ingredients in a measuring jug and cook on HIGH for 2 to 3 minutes, stirring every minute.

Serve with sponge puddings or vanilla ice cream.
Makes 175ml (6 fl oz)

Jam Sauce: Replace the marmalade with jam and proceed as above. Sieve if necessary before serving.

CHOCOLATE FUDGE SAUCE

50 g (2 oz) plain
    chocolate
50 g (2 oz) butter
4 tablespoons evaporated
    milk
75 g (3 oz) caster sugar
1 teaspoon vanilla essence

Place the chocolate and butter in a measuring jug and cook on HIGH for about 2 minutes or until melted, stirring after 1 minute. Stir in the milk and sugar and beat until creamy and smooth. Stir in the vanilla essence. Reheat on HIGH for 30 to 45 seconds if necessary.

Serve with ice cream or fruit.
Makes 175 ml (6 fl oz)

POURING EGG CUSTARD SAUCE

300 ml (½ pint) milk
2 egg yolks
25 g (1 oz) caster sugar
vanilla essence

Place the milk in a measuring jug and heat on HIGH for 2 minutes.

Beat the egg yolks and sugar together in a bowl. Gradually stir in the heated milk. Cook on HIGH for about 2 minutes, stirring every 30 seconds. Stir in vanilla essence to taste.
Makes 300 ml (½ pint)
NOTE: For a thicker custard, blend 15 g (½ oz) cornflour with the milk before heating.

THREE FRUIT MARMALADE

2 grapefruit
2 oranges
2 lemons
900 ml (1½ pints) boiling
  water
2 kg (4 lb) preserving or
  granulated sugar

Cut all the fruit in half, squeeze the juice and set aside. Remove the pips and white pith from the rinds and tie in a piece of muslin. Shred the peel coarsely or finely, as preferred. Place the juice, peel and muslin bag in a large bowl and add 300 ml (½ pint) of the water. Leave to stand overnight.

Remove the muslin bag and add the remaining boiling water. Cover and cook on HIGH for 20 to 30 minutes, depending on the thickness of the peel, until the peel is soft.

Add the sugar and stir until dissolved. Cook, uncovered, on HIGH for 25 to 35 minutes or until setting point is reached; stir every 5 minutes and test for setting frequently after 20 minutes (see below). Leave to stand for 15 to 20 minutes to cool slightly, then stir and pour into sterilized warmed jars. Cover, seal and label in the usual way.
Makes 2.5 kg (5½ lb)

STRAWBERRY JAM

500 g (1 lb) strawberries,
  hulled
1 tablespoon lemon juice
375 g (12 oz) preserving
  or granulated sugar

Place the strawberries and lemon juice in a large bowl, at least 2.75 litre (5 pint) capacity. Cover and cook on HIGH for 5 to 6 minutes, until soft.

Add the sugar and stir gently until dissolved. Cook on HIGH, uncovered, for 12 to 15 minutes, until setting point is reached; test for setting frequently after 10 minutes (see below).

Leave to cool slightly then stir and pour into sterilized warmed jars. Cover, seal and label in the usual way.
Makes about 750 g (1½ lb)

To test for set: Boil to 104°C (220°F), using a sugar thermometer to check the temperature. Or, place 1 teaspoon jam on a saucer and leave to cool. When setting point is reached, a skin will form which wrinkles when pushed with a finger.

SIX-MINUTE LEMON CURD

75 g (3 oz) butter
250 g (8 oz) caster sugar
3 eggs
finely grated rind and juice
of 2 lemons

Melt the butter in a 1.5 litre (2½ pint) bowl on HIGH for about 1½ minutes.

Beat together the sugar, eggs, lemon rind and juice. Stir into the melted butter, mixing well.

Cook on HIGH for about 3 minutes, or until the mixture coats the back of a spoon. Stir every 30 seconds, stirring very briskly as the mixture starts to thicken, to keep it smooth.

Pour into small warmed jars, cover, seal and label in the usual way. Store in a refrigerator for up to 2 weeks.
Makes about 500 g (1 lb)

DATE AND APPLE CHUTNEY

750 g (1½ lb) cooking
apples, peeled, cored
and chopped
500 g (1 lb) stoned dates,
chopped
250 g (8 oz) onions,
finely chopped
250 g (8 oz) soft dark
brown sugar
125 g (4 oz) sultanas
1 teaspoon salt
1 teaspoon ground ginger
½ teaspoon cayenne
pepper
600 ml (1 pint) malt
vinegar

Place all the ingredients in a large
bowl, cover and cook on HIGH for
35 to 45 minutes or until thickened,
stirring every 10 minutes.

Leave to cool slightly, then ladle
into sterilized warmed jars. Cover,
seal and label in the usual way.
Makes about 2 kg (4½ lb)

TOMATO CHUTNEY

750 g (1½ lb) tomatoes,
skinned and quartered
250 g (8 oz) onions,
finely chopped
125 g (4 oz) soft dark
brown sugar
125 g (4 oz) sultanas
1 teaspoon salt
1 teaspoon ground mixed
spice
½ teaspoon cayenne
pepper
300 ml (½ pint) malt
vinegar

Place all the ingredients in a large
bowl, cover and cook on HIGH for
35 to 45 minutes or until thickened,
stirring every 10 minutes.

Leave to cool slightly, then ladle
into sterilized warmed jars. Cover,
seal and label in the usual way.
Makes about 1.5 kg (3-3½ lb)

RHUBARB CHUTNEY

500 g (1 lb) rhubarb,
chopped
500 g (1 lb) stoned dates,
chopped
1 large onion, chopped
125 g (4 oz) soft dark
brown sugar
300 ml (½ pint) spiced
vinegar

Place all the ingredients in a very
large bowl and mix well. Cover and
cook on HIGH for about 30 minutes
or until thickened, stirring every
10 minutes.

Leave to cool slightly, then ladle
into sterilized warmed jars. Cover,
seal and label in the usual way.
Makes 1-1.5 kg (2-3½ lb)

ENTERTAINING DISHES

VICHYSSOISE

500 g (1 lb) leeks
1 kg (2 lb) potatoes
*1 litre (1¾ pints) boiling
  chicken stock*
*250 ml (8 fl oz) single
  cream*
salt and pepper
chopped chives to garnish

Thinly slice the white part and about a third of the green part of leeks and place in a large casserole with the potatoes.

Add the stock, cover and cook on HIGH for about 10 minutes or until the potatoes are tender.

Work in an electric blender or food processor until smooth. Stir in the cream, and season with salt and pepper to taste. Chill thoroughly.

Garnish with chopped chives to serve.
Serves 6

STUFFED TOMATOES

6 tomatoes
50 g (2 oz) tongue, chopped
40 g (1½ oz) smooth liver pâté
2 tablespoons chopped parsley
3 tablespoons dried breadcrumbs
1 tablespoon single cream or top of the milk
salt and pepper
cayenne pepper
parsley sprigs to garnish

Slice the tops from the tomatoes and set aside. Carefully spoon out the flesh and mix with the remaining ingredients, seasoning with salt, pepper and cayenne to taste.

Fill the tomatoes with the mixture and replace the tops to form lids. Arrange in a circle around the edge of a round dish and cook on HIGH for 6 to 9 minutes, until just tender. Serve hot, garnished with parsley and accompanied by toast.

Serves 6

CHICKEN LIVER PÂTÉ

500 g (1 lb) chicken livers
450 ml (¾ pint) chicken stock
2 tablespoons chopped onion
50 g (2 oz) butter, softened
2 tablespoons mayonnaise
2 tablespoons brandy
1 teaspoon celery salt
pinch of dry mustard
pinch of ground mixed spice
4 bay leaves
TO SERVE:
cranberry sauce
hot toast

Pierce the chicken livers with a fork and place in a deep casserole with the stock and onion. Cover and cook on HIGH for 6 to 8 minutes or until boiling. Stir well, cover and cook on LOW for 2 to 3 minutes or until the livers are only slightly pink in the centres; do not overcook.

Remove the liver and onion with a slotted spoon and place in an electric blender or food processor. Work until smooth, then add the butter, mayonnaise, brandy, celery salt, mustard and spice and blend until smooth.

Arrange the bay leaves in the base of an oiled 600 ml (1 pint) mould or dish and place the liver mixture on top. Cover with foil and leave in the refrigerator overnight.

Dip the mould or dish in hot water and turn the pâté out onto a serving plate. Serve with cranberry sauce and hot toast.
Serves 6 to 8

CHICKEN CACCIATORE

1 × 397 g (14 oz) can tomatoes
1 × 142 g (5 oz) can tomato purée
120 ml (4 fl oz) dry white wine
1 clove garlic, crushed
1 teaspoon dried oregano
salt
4-6 chicken portions
1 large onion, sliced
TO GARNISH:
lemon twists
parsley sprigs

Place the tomatoes with their juice, tomato purée, wine, garlic, oregano, and salt to taste in a jug and mix well.

Arrange the chicken portions in a casserole, skin side down and meatiest portions towards the outside of the dish. Add the onion rings and pour over the tomato mixture.

Cover and cook on HIGH for 15 minutes. Turn the chicken portions over, rearrange, cover and cook on HIGH for 10 to 15 minutes, until the chicken is tender and the juices run clear. Leave to stand, covered, for 5 minutes.

Garnish with lemon twists and parsley sprigs. Serve with boiled rice.
Serves 4 to 6

PIQUANT PORK CHOPS

4 loin pork chops, 1 cm
   (½ inch) thick
Worcestershire sauce
125 g (4 oz) red Cheddar
   or Cheshire cheese,
   grated
2 tablespoons single cream
1 tablespoon Dijon
   mustard
chopped chives to garnish

Brush the chops sparingly on both
sides with Worcestershire sauce.
Arrange in a single layer in a dish,
with the meatiest portions towards
the outside.

Cover and cook on HIGH for
5 minutes. Reduce to LOW and
continue cooking for 20 to
22 minutes, draining the chops after
10 minutes.

Mix together the cheese, cream and
mustard and spread over the chops.
Cook on HIGH for about 2 minutes
or until the cheese has melted.

Sprinkle with chopped chives and
serve immediately with sauté
potatoes and broccoli spears.
Serves 4

POACHED SALMON STEAKS

4 × 175 g (6 oz) salmon
    steaks
juice of ½ lemon
pepper
120 ml (4 fl oz) white
    wine
TO GARNISH:
lemon twists
parsley sprigs

Arrange the salmon steaks in a
shallow dish, with the meatiest
portions towards the outside.
Sprinkle with the lemon juice, and
pepper to taste, and pour over the
wine.

Cover and cook on HIGH for 7 to
8 minutes, or until the centre of the
fish is just beginning to flake when
tested with a fork; turn the steaks
over after 4 minutes and rotate the
dish if the oven does not have a
turntable.

Leave to stand, covered, for
5 minutes, then garnish with lemon
twists and parsley sprigs. Serve hot
with new potatoes and hollandaise
sauce, or serve cold with mayonnaise
and salad.
Serves 4

ORANGE-GLAZED GAMMON

1 × 2 kg (4½ lb)
  unsmoked gammon
  joint, soaked in cold
  water overnight
grated rind and juice of
  1 orange
2-3 tablespoons clear
  honey
75-125 g (3-4 oz)
  demerara sugar

Drain the gammon and dry thoroughly. Weigh the joint and calculate the cooking time, allowing 7 minutes per 500 g (1 lb). Tie securely with string, place in a pierced roasting bag and tie the end with string. Place on a *microwave roasting rack*, or an upturned plate in a dish. Cook on HIGH for half the calculated cooking time. Leave to stand for 15 minutes.

Place the orange juice, rind and honey in a small bowl and cook on HIGH for 2 minutes to heat through. Remove the skin from the gammon, score the fat in a diamond pattern and brush with half the orange mixture.

Roll the joint in the sugar and replace it in the roasting bag. Place it the other side up on the rack or plate and cook on HIGH for the remaining cooking time or until a meat thermometer registers 70°C (160°F). Leave to stand for 10 minutes in the roasting bag. Brush with the remaining glaze and leave to cool.

Serve cold with an orange and watercress salad.
Serves 6

RASPBERRY CREAM GÂTEAU

150 g (5 oz) self-raising
  flour
25 g (1 oz) cornflour
pinch of salt
150 g (5 oz) caster sugar
2 eggs, separated
4 tablespoons warm water
2 tablespoons corn oil
few drops of vanilla
  essence
TO FINISH:
350 g (12 oz) frozen
  raspberries, thawed
284 ml (10 fl oz) double
  cream, whipped

Sift the flour, cornflour, salt and sugar into a bowl. Beat the egg yolks and stir in the water, oil and vanilla essence. Stir into the dry ingredients. Whisk the egg whites until stiff and fold into the mixture.

Divide between two greased 18 cm (7 inch) cake dishes. Cook one at a time on HIGH for about 4 minutes. Leave to stand for 5 minutes before turning out onto a wire rack to cool. Chill for 1 hour.

Cut each sponge in half. Sandwich the layers together with raspberries and cream, reserving some for the top.
Serves 8

PINEAPPLE À LA CRÈME

1 × 439 g (15½ oz) can
  pineapple pieces in
  natural juice
50 g (2 oz) cornflour
3 tablespoons caster sugar
  or to taste
few drops of vanilla
  essence
284 ml (10 fl oz) double
  cream, whipped

Drain the pineapple and set aside. Make up the juice to 600 ml (1 pint) with water, and pour into a large serving bowl. Blend in the cornflour, then stir in the sugar. Cook on HIGH for 6 minutes, stirring frequently. Stir in the vanilla essence and leave to cool.

Reserve 5 tablespoons of the cream and fold the remainder into the cornflour mixture. Fold in the pineapple, reserving a few pieces for decoration. Chill until set. Decorate with cream rosettes and pineapple.
Serves 4

CHOCOLATE MOUSSE

125 g (4 oz) plain
  chocolate
15 g (½ oz) butter,
  softened
4 eggs, separated
1 tablespoon rum
TO DECORATE:
120 ml (4 fl oz) whipping
  cream, whipped
25 g (1 oz) plain
  chocolate, grated

Break the chocolate into small pieces and place in a bowl with the butter. Cook on HIGH for 2 minutes until melted, stirring after 1 minute. Stir in the beaten egg yolks and rum. Whisk the egg whites until stiff and fold into the mixture. Pour into 4 to 6 individual dishes and chill until set.

Decorate with whipped cream and grated chocolate to serve.
Serves 4 to 6

INDEX